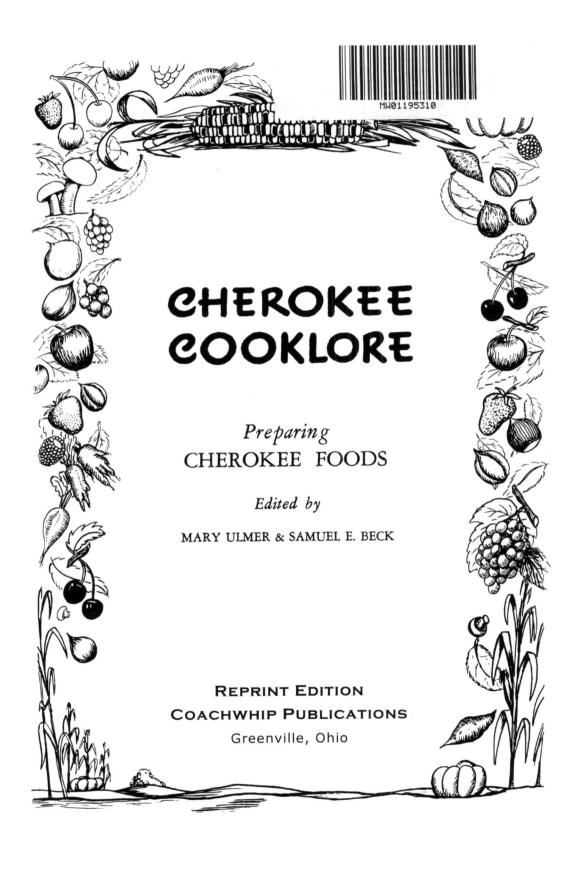

CHEROKEE COOKLORE

Preparing
CHEROKEE FOODS

Edited by

MARY ULMER & SAMUEL E. BECK

REPRINT EDITION

COACHWHIP PUBLICATIONS

Greenville, Ohio

Cherokee Cooklore: Preparing Cherokee Foods
© 2014 Coachwhip Publications
First published 1951 by Mary and Goingback Chiltoskey for the Museum of
    the Cherokee Indian. No renewal.
No claims made on public domain material.

CoachwhipBooks.com

ISBN 1-61646-257-4
ISBN-13 978-1-61646-257-4

INTRODUCTION

THE AMERICAN INDIAN'S greatest contribution to our civilization is, in the eyes of many experts, the patient cultivation from their original wild state of the food plants which are now more than half our agricultural wealth.

The Museum wanted to preserve these recipes as a permanent tribute to the Cherokees; also the many guests at our Annual Feasts have asked for them. We were fortunate in persuading Miss Mary Ulmer, teacher at the Reservation School and a loved, respected and welcome guest in Reservation homes, to undertake the considerable research. Her task has been admirably accomplished.

These recipes are rich in folklore, retaining the quaint mystery with which the forbears of the present-day Cherokees endowed them. These men and women found the fullness of life in quiet woodlands, giving gratitude and adoration to the Great Spirit for sustenance.

Samuel E Beck

FOUNDER

MUSEUM OF THE CHEROKEE INDIAN

Drawings by Goingback Chiltoskey. Photos of Aggie Lossiah by Juanita Wilson

Aggie Lossiah, grand-daughter of Chief John Ross, demonstrates the fine art of bean bread making, "just like my Cherokee granny made it when we lived in that cave on the Tennessee River."

"Sure, corn meal is the main part of bean bread. Corn meal is the main part of the food eaten by us Indians. Beans are used, too. If you folks will visit with me for a while I'll show you how bean bread ought to be made. How my old Cherokee granny made it when we lived in that cave on the Tennessee River, only I have a few pots and pans like my old granny never had. Maybe I'll give you a taste of some that I cooked yesterday, if you want it."

"You passed my corn patch yonder as you came up the mountain. That's flour corn, the best kind to eat. Right in that patch is where I gathered this corn I'm going to use."

"My old Big Cove friend, Mollie Runningwolfe, gave me these beans."

"I'll set the beans to cooking here by the fire in the fireplace whilst we go out to the branch to skin the corn."

"Pour some water into this iron pot here over the fire."

"Sift in some good wood ashes."

12

"Pour in the shelled corn."

''Stir once in a while and let cook
until the bubbles begin to come up.''

''Take out a grain to test it with the fingers to see if the skin is ready to slip. That is the way we tell if it has been in the lye water long enough.''

19

"Wash the corn in a basket seive to get rid of the skins."

"Put the corn into the wooden beater (Ka No Na) and beat it with a heavy piece of wood. Yes, use the little end; the big end is to give weight."

''Feel the meal to see if it is fine
enough.''

"The hot beans and their soup are poured into the pan of meal. No, leave out the salt. Work quickly so the mixture will not get cold."

"Work the mixture into a ball."

"Flatten the ball because we are making 'b r o a d s w o r d s', as my granddaddy called them. Not John Ross, but my other granddaddy. You know I had two of them. "

31

"Wrap the corn blades around the dumpling. The blades were pulled green and hung up by the little end to dry, then scalded to make limber. Fold the ends under to hold or tie with a strong grass. We'll cook these in the iron pot out by the branch. The clear water I left out there should be boiling by now. "

33

"The bean dumplings will have to boil about an hour so I shall let you try one of these that I cooked yesterday. The only difference is that I wrapped them in oak leaves."

‘‘I know you want some.’’

"What about you? Some people do not like them the first time but after a few times you will like them as well as she does."

"Grandpap, you should have seen the look on that man's face when I handed him that piece of my good bean bread."

In Memoriam

AGGIE ROSS LOSSIAH

Dec. 22, 1880 - Jan. 20, 1966

Where These Recipes Came From

THE recipes and directions for cooking some of the foods enjoyed by the Eastern Cherokee Indians of North Carolina contained in this pamphlet were secured from the Cherokee Indians during the years 1949 and 1950. In each case the person giving the information was either well over three score years or had learned the older methods from foreparents. The women are known in their communities as "good Indian cooks" and the men have "well-fed" appearances.

Section One is made up of information obtained from Aggie Lossiah who before her marriage to Henry Lossiah was Aggie Ross, granddaughter of John Ross. John Ross was the Principal Chief of the Cherokee Nation at the time of the Removal in the 1830's. Aggie's almost 70 years have carried her over a long and interesting trail to the present-day civilization. During three years of her childhood she made her home with some relatives who lived in a cave along the banks of the Little Tennessee River across from the present town of Calderwood, Tenn. Today Aggie lives in a comfortable mountainside home near the village of Cherokee where she feeds her family and friends on good Indian food with an occasional dish of "white man's food" served to add variety.

The recipes in Section Two were given by Mrs. Katie Taylor Brady of the Birdtown community. Mrs. Brady had the excellent training of her grandmother in learning to prepare Indian foods. Her rather modern kitchen, with its electric refrigerator and large wood stove, is often the scene of the preparation of good bean dumplings as well as other excellent foods.

Mrs. Wayne Tahquette inherited from her mother the oft-tried recipes given in Section Three. Many visitors to the campus of the Cherokee Indian School get their first taste of Indian food in the kitchen of this good cook.

Mrs. Clifford Hornbuckle, who had the training of her mother and grandmother to help her become what is often spoken of by many of the Cherokees as being the best cook who can cook both Indian and "white man's" food, gave the recipes in Section Four.

And the men are not ignorant of the knowledge of how to prepare the food of their foreparents. William Crowe and Goingback Chiltoskey spent an interesting evening reminiscing over the good Indian foods that an excellent cook—the mother of Goingback and the grandmother of William—prepared to satisfy their growing appetites in the years that had passed. Section Five is the result of their session of "remembering."

The very size of Jim Will readily tells anyone that he has been well fed. The recipes in Section Six were given by him. He learned from his mother the fine art of food preparation and added to it much knowledge gained from several years in the Navy.

Agnes Catolster (Mrs. Johnson Catolster) gave the one recipe in Section Seven. She knows and uses many others. She readily agreed with her husband that he taught her to cook many of the Indian dishes. Those who have had the privilege of eating her food are sure that she was an excellent pupil with the best kind of teacher.

Mollie Runningwolfe Sequoyah took great pride in telling how she and many others in Big Cove prepare good food. Mollie is one of the older cooks who has passed her art of cooking to many of her neighbors. She gave the recipes in Section Eight.

The compiler of these recipes has had the privilege of eating much good Cherokee foods (including Ramps) in many homes but the biggest thrill came from being allowed to make bean bread in the home of Mrs. Watty Chiltoskie. All of the Cherokee foods are not by any means contained in the pamphlet but surely some of the best are included. All the good cooks are not mentioned but it is hoped that their art will be preserved a little better because of this little attempt at putting some of them into print. The world would surely be devoid of some of its best food if the Cherokee way of cooking should suddenly disappear.

It is hoped that the reader will not be disturbed by the absence of exact measurements—any really good cook is apt to fall into the use of such terms as "a dash of this and a pinch of that", so naturally being good cooks, the Cherokees give their directions in a general manner assuming that one who likes to cook has that special something that acts as a guide in such matters.

To the memory of those good Cherokee cooks of a destitute period of the past when subsistence living was the only living, this little pamphlet is lovingly dedicated with the hope that we who are younger will be able to do just half as well if we are faced with the same situation.

Cherokee, North Carolina

March, 1951.

MARY ULMER, compiler

BEAN BREAD—Tsu-Ya-Ga Du— ᏍᏏ ᏚᏫ

The Cherokee people made bread before the white man came along with his mills for grinding corn into meal or his soda for making the bread rise. To prepare meal to make Bean Bread one uses flour corn. This corn is skinned with wood ashes. Sieve the ashes, put these ashes into an iron pot or well-made pottery over the fire. When the water begins to boil put in the corn, stir once in a while to make sure that the corn does not stick. Let this boil until it is thick enough to bubble. Take the corn off the fire. Go to the branch, or whatever source of water that is nearby, wash the corn in the running water by placing it in a sieve and letting the water run through it until it is clean. The sieve is a basket that is made so that there will be little holes in the bottom to let the water go through. After washing the corn let it drip until all extra water is dropped off it. While the corn is still damp pound it into meal by using the old homemade corn beater. This beater is made by hollowing out a log or stump and beating with a pole with the piece the size of the tree left at the top to give it weight.

To make the Bean Bread, boil dry beans in plain water until tender. Pour boiling beans and some of the soup into the cornmeal and stir until mixed. Have pot of plain water on the fire boiling. If you want bean dumplings, just make mixture out in balls and cook in the pot of plain water, uncovered, until done. Eat these dumplings plain, with butter, meat grease (the Indian's favorite), wild game, hot or cold, as suits one's fancy. If you want broadswords you should mold the dumplings flat in the hand and wrap in corn blades, cured corn fodder, or hickory, oak or cucumber tree leaves. Tie with a stout reed unless able to tie the wrappings. Drop this into the boiling water, cover, and boil until done. Do not put any salt in Bean Bread or it will crumble.

CURING FODDER

Gather even lengths of broad mature blades from the corn plant. Gather the point ends together, double over and tie. Hang in the shade to dry for winter use. Dip in hot water to limber up when ready to use.

BEAN BREAD—after advent of grist mills.

Use fine corn meal that has been ground at the grist mill. Sieve the meal, add wood ashes lye to the meal until it begins to turn a little yellow. Add cooked beans, soup and all while boiling hot. Proceed from here as in the first recipe.

BEAN BREAD—Modern

Use any kind of cornmeal, add cooked beans, baking soda and salt. Cook in a pan as ordinary cornbread. Eat hot or cold but do not be surprised if it is not very good. The salt will make the bread crumble so it cannot be made into very good dumplings or broadswords.

WOOD ASHES LYE

Put hardwood ashes into a bucket, barrel, old piece of pottery, or any container that has holes in the bottom. Pour water over the ashes, catch the drippings in any kind of vessel except a tin one or an aluminum one. Pottery and gourds are good for catching the lye drippings. Wood ashes lye is very strong and care should be taken in handling it.

WALNUT MIXTURE—Se-Di A-Su-Yi   ᏎᏗ ᎠᏑᏯ

Skin and wash some flour corn the same as for Bean Bread. Put the corn into a pot, cook until the grains begin to crack, add raw shelled beans (also pumpkin if you have it and like it), cook until beans are soft. While this is cooking prepare walnut meats by pounding them in the corn beater, then mixing with a little water. Add this to the cooking mixture, stir constantly while cooking for 10 or 15 minutes more, or until done. A little meal may be added with the walnut meats to make it thicken.

CHESTNUT BREAD—Di-S-Qua-Ni   ᎠᏍᏆᏂ

Prepare the meal the same as for Bean Bread but use chestnuts instead of beans. Cut the chestnuts in small pieces before cooking them.

SWEET POTATO BREAD—Oo-Ga-Na-S-Ti Nu-Nv Ga-Du

Prepare the same as for Bean Bread but use pieces
of cooked but not over-cooked sweet potatoes.

CARROT BREAD   ᏓᏌᎦᏫᏗ ᏄᏅ ᎦᏚ

Prepare the same as for Bean Bread but use pieces
of carrots not too well cooked.

PARCHED CORN MEAL—Gv-Wi Si-Da   ᎬᎤ ᏏᏓ

Use flour corn if you have some. Sieve ashes into an
oven (the kind used for cooking out of doors on the fire or
in the house on the fireplace), set over coals to keep hot,
stir ashes until really hot, place corn in the hot ashes and
stir until grains of corn are evenly browned. Sift ashes
off, put the corn into the corn beater and pound into meal.
Sift the meal from the grits. Use this meal as food on a
hunting trip. It may be mixed with molasses, honey or
sugar. It may be eaten dry or mixed with water. The
grits sifted out may be used for hominy soup.

HOMINY SOUP—Gv-Wi Si-Da A-Ma-Gi-I ᎬᎤ Ꮟ ᎠᎹᎩᎢ

Put grits left from sieving parched cornmeal into
boiling water. Cook briskly until soft, pour this into a
storage vessel. Drink fresh, hot or cold, or wait for it
to ferment.

HOMINY SOUP—Gv-No-He-Nv A-Ma-Gi-I ᎬᏃᎮᏅ ᎠᎹᎩᎢ

Put wood ashes lye into a pot, add water, bring to boil.
Add corn and stir until grains turn yellow. Pour into sieve
basket to remove excess lye. Pound grains in corn beater
until all grains are cracked several times. Sieve this
cracked corn to remove bran. Winnowing in flat baskets
was often used by the old Indians for removing the bran.
Make the soup as when using parched corn grits.

BARBECUED MEAT—A-Su-Nv Ta-Na-Yv ᎠᏑᏅ ᏔᎾᏴ

Cut meat into small blocks or strips. String these
pieces on a sharpened stick, place before a hot fire, turn
often until meat quits dripping. Remove meat from stick
and string it on a bark thong or bear grass and hang before or above the fireplace for future use. When ready to
use this meat it may be made into a stew just as it is or

it may be pounded in the corn beater until soft and then cooked as a soup. If the meat is tough it is best to pound it. Use only a little salt for seasoning.

BARBECUED FISH—A-Su-Nv Ta-A A-Gu-Di DᏉᏩ ᎳᎠ ᎠᏧᎫ

Cut fish into strips of chunks, string on pieces of sharpened sticks and hang over or before a fire. Turn often and keep before the fire until fish does not drip any more. Hang up for later by stringing on thongs, bear grass, etc. Use by making stew or soup.

VEGETABLES—So-Cha-Ni ᏒᏣᏫᏂ
SWEET GRASS—Oo-Ga-Na-S-Di ᎤᎦᏁᏍᏗ
OLD FIELD CREASES—Oo-Li-Si ᎤᎵᏂ
RAMPS—Wa-S-Di ᎳᏍᏗ ANGELICA—Wa-Ne-Gi-Dun ᎳᏁᎩᏚᏅ
BEAN SALAD—Gu-Hi-Tli-Gi ᎫᎮᏟᎩ POKE—Tla-Ye-De ᏝᏤᏕ

These are some of the early spring plants that the Cherokee people have eaten for as long back as any of us know about and are still enjoyed by many today. These plants may be cooked together or separately. Usually they are parboiled, salted, cooked some more with grease, if available, then served.

MUSHROOMS—Di-Wa-Li ᏗᎳᎵ

Mushrooms are gathered by those fortunate enough to know the good ones. They are parboiled, fried, made into soup, eaten with butter or grease, or other ways that the eater might fancy.

SASSAFRAS TEA—Ga-Na-S-Da-Tsi ᎦᏁᏍᏓᏥ

Gather and wash the roots of the red sassafras. Do this in the early spring before the sap rises. Store for future use. When ready to make tea, boil a few pieces of the roots, serve hot. Sweeten if desired.

SPICEWOOD TEA—Gv-Nv-S-Dv-Tli ᎬᏅᏍᏛᏟ

Gather small twigs when the first buds appear, boil in water, serve hot. Sweeten if desired, molasses makes the best sweetening.

HICKORY NUT SOUP—Ga-Nu-Ge ᏍᏊᎱ

Gather hickory nuts or scalybarks, dry on a rack before the fire. When the nuts are dry crack them by using a large flat rock placed in a flat basket lined temporarily with a cloth, use a smaller rock to pound the nuts when placed on the larger rock. When the nuts are all cracked sieve them through a sieve basket. Place the kernels and small hulls that passed through the sieve in the corn beater and pound until the substance can be made into balls. Roll this into balls until ready for use. These balls will keep fresh for several days if the weather is not too warm.

When ready for Hickory Nut Soup place a ball or more in a vessel that will hold water, pour boiling water over the balls while stirring constantly. If this is made into a thick soup it may be served with any type bread or dumpling. If it is made into a thin soup it may be used as a drink. As soon as enough soup has been poured off to leave a very thick mixture more water may be added. Do not drink the very last of the mixture because that is where the little bits of hulls are.

POSSUM GRAPE DRINK—Oo-Ni-Na-Su-Ga Oo-Ga-Ma ᎤᏂᎾᏑᎦ ᎤᎦᎹ

Gather ripe possum grapes--the kind that are still sour after they ripen when the frost has fallen on them-- hang up for winter use. To prepare, shell off the grapes from the stems, wash, stew them in water. When they are done mash in the water in which they were cooked, let this sit until the seeds settle, then pour off the juice. Put the juice back on the fire, when boiling add a little cornmeal to thicken, continue cooking until the meal is done. Remove from the fire and drink hot or cold.

OLD FIELD APRICOT DRINK—Oo-Wa-Ga ᎤᏩᎦ

Gather old field apricots--the fruit of the Passion Flower. Hull out the seeds and pulp, put these on to boil after adding a tiny bit of soda to make the seeds separate from the pulp. Strain the juice from the seeds and pulp, add meal to the juice and cook until the meal is done.

DRIED APPLES—Oo-Ni-Ka-Yo-Sv-I Sv-Ga-Ta ᎣᏂᎧᏲᏒᎢ ᏒᎦᏔ

Gather the ripe apples, peel and core, string on white oak splits, place before the fire but not too close, turn them often. When they are dry store by hanging across the rafters of the cabin for future use. When ready to use, remove from splits, wash and stew.

DRIED CABBAGE—Oo-Ka-Yo-Sv-I S-Que-Wi ᎣᎧᏲᏒᎢ ᏍᏇᏫ

When removing outside leaves of cabbage to make kraut, or to use for other things, string these outside leaves on a stick and hang in the sun or warm place to dry. Drying in the house often makes the leaves more tender than drying in the sun. To prepare for eating, remove from the sticks, pour hot water over them, wash, put in clean water and boil until tender. This may be seasoned with grease and salt if desired. Eat with lye corn dumplings.

LYE DUMPLINGS—Di-Gu-Nv-I ᏗᎫᏅᎢ

Mix enough wood ashes lye with meal to make it begin to turn yellow, add boiling water to make it to a mixture that will easily form small balls or pones. Make balls and drop into boiling water, cook until done. Do not add salt lest they crumble. Serve hot. Grease may be poured over them for seasoning.

GINGERBREAD-LOOKING MUSHOOMS—Di-Wa-Li Oo-Ni-Wa-Di-Ge-I ᏗᏩᎵ ᎣᏂᏩᏗᎨᎢ

Gather the mushrooms and wash thoroughly. Rake out fire coals, lay mushrooms on the coals, sprinkle with salt, turn over until well done. Eat with bread or dumplings. In later years when it has been easier to get grease some of the Indians fry these mushrooms in grease. The ones cooked on the coals are the best.

SLICK-GO-DOWNS—Oo-Ni-Lo-Que ᎣᏂᎶᏇ

Gather these mushrooms as soon as they come up because after they begin to get brown they are not very good. Parboil, pour off water, salt and add fresh water and grease if desired. Boil until done. Serve with cornmeal mush. Eat by dipping up a spoon of mush and a spoon of the soup or pour the soup over the mush.

WISI—Wi-Si ᏫᏏ

Gather this type of mushroom, strip it into small bits, parboil, drain off water, stew in fresh water until tender. Eat as is with bread or mush, or fry in grease.

ASH CAKE

Make a stiff dough of cornmeal and warm water. Rake ashes back, spread hot stone of bottom of fireplace or outdoor cooking place with oak leaves, put pone of bread on the leaves, cover with more leaves and pile on red-hot ashes. Remove pone when done. Eat in any manner that bread is eaten.

CORN BREAD BAKED ON BARK

When traveling the Cherokees were not able to carry their cooking utensils so they had to improvise on such occasions. When it was time to cook bread one of the men would carefully cut pieces of bark from a chestnut tree. The dough was put on the inside of the bark and this was stood up before the fire to cook. The combination of bark, wood smoke and hunger made this bread about the best any Indian ever ate.

FLAT DUMPLINGS

Beat meal as for other types of bread. Make dumplings rather thin, boil in plain water until done. Let cool, aplit open and put in flat basket to run over the flames of the fire. This basket of split dumplings was passed over the flame four times, once each to the North, East, South and West, to keep the skillies off. Then the basket was set outside to freeze. Eat the frozen bread in the morning while it is still frozen. The smoke left a very pleasant flavor to the bread. Any cold bread could be done this way. Old people especially got lots of pleasure from sitting by a good fire on an icy day slowly munching on a bit of frozen bread while telling the younger ones about the olden days.

FROGS (TOADS)—Wi-Lo-Si ᏪᏝᏏ

Catch toads, twist off their heads, pull off the skin while all the time holding the animals under running water lest the meat become very bitter. Parboil, then cook as any other meat.

KNEE-DEEPS—Du-S-Du ᏚᏍᏚ

Catch early frogs--called Knee-Deeps--scald and skin. Parboil and cook like other meats.

DEERHORN MUSHROOMS

Pick this kind of mushroom, wash, tear apart and parboil until tender. Fry this in a little grease and eat as a vegetable.

SECTION TWO

FISH AND MUSH

Barbecue fish by cooking it on a stick, after being cut into small chunks, boil in water to make a thick soup. Make mush by cooking cornmeal with a little lye or soda and water. Eat the mush with the fish soup. This dish was always used for sick people when they had fish.

LEATHER BREECHES—A-Ni-Ka-Yo-Sv-Hi Tsu-Ya ᎠᏂᎧᏲᏒᎯ ᏧᏯ

Gather green beans as soon as the beans in the pods mature. Break off the ends and string the pods on a thread or lay them out in a single layer on a sheet. Put the beans in the sun for several days to dry, bringing them into the house at night and during rainy weather. Store for future use by hanging from the rafters or the wall. When ready for use, soak the beans overnight and cook all day the next day. Salt and grease may be put in them while they are cooking if available and desired.

SWEET BREAD—Oo-Ga-Na-S-Di Ga-Du ᎤᎦᎾᏍᏗ ᎦᏚ

Make a dough from flour just like making biscuits. Add some molasses, sugar or honey. Bake this in small or large pones, just as you like. Eat this as you would cake.

51

BAKED APPLES—Sv-Ga-Ta   R𒀱W
Pick ripe apples. Cover the apples with hot ashes
and live coals, cook until as soft as you want them.

DRIED CORN—Se-Lu Ka-Yo-Tuv-Nu-Hl 4M ᎤᏏᎦᎤᎠ
Gather corn in the roasting ear stage. Strip shucks
back and tie, hang this in the sun for several days until
the grains are dry. Store the dried corn by hanging from
the rafters or the wall. To prepare for eating, soak the
corn and then shell it from the cob. Cook the grains by
boiling. This may be seasoned the same as green corn.

SECTION THREE

POTATO SOUP—Nu-Nv Oo-Ga-Ma   ᏋᏫᎤ ᎤᏍᎧ
Peel white potatoes and cut them into small pieces.
Boil in water with an onion or two until potatoes and
onions mash easily. After mashing add some fresh milk
and reheat the mixture. Add salt and pepper if desired.
This soup is best when eaten hot.

CABBAGE—S-Que-Wi   ᏲᏫᎾ
Wilt cabbage in a small amount of grease, add some
pieces of green peppers and cook until the cabbage turns
red. Serve this with cornbread.

SECTION FOUR

HOMINY CORN DRINK—Gv-No-He-Nv   ᎡᏃᎮᏫᎤ
Shell corn, soak in lye until the skin can be removed.
Beat the corn in the corn beater until it is the size of
hominy. Sift the meal from the corn particles. Cook the
corn particles until they are done, thicken this a little
with meal. Drink this hot or wait until it sours and drink
it cold. The drink may be kept for quite a while unless
the weather is very hot. This was the customary drink to
serve to friends who dropped by for a visit.

Ga-Nu-Ge   ᏍᏴᏞ
Crack thin shelled hickory nuts, beat hull and all in

the corn beater until it can be rolled into a ball. Make size balls that are convenient to use. Pour boiling water over this to make a thick gruel. Pour this over corn and beans that have been mixed after being cooked separately. If made thin is good to serve as a drink.

CORN AND BEANS—Se-Lu A-Su-Yi Tu-Ya 4M DᏉᎶ ᎫᏔ

Skin flour corn with lye. Cook. Cook colored beans. Put the cooked corn and beans together and cook some more, add pumpkin if you like it. If you add pumpkin cook until the pumpkin is done. Add to this a mixture of cornmeal, beaten walnuts and hickory nuts, and enough molasses to sweeten. Cook this in an iron pot until the meal is done. Eat fresh or after it begins to sour. This will not keep too long after it begins to sour unless the weather is cold.

FRIED CORN AND BEANS

Cook skinned corn and colored beans separately, then put together and cook some more. Add a little grease and set aside to cool. When firm fry in hot grease.

CHICKEN AND CORN—Tsi-Ta-Ga A-Su-Yi Se-Lu ᏏᏔᏍ DᏉᎶ 4M

Stew chicken until well done, add cooked skinned corn, cook together enough to get a good flavor. Beans may be added if you like. Season to taste with salt and pepper.

DRIED CABBAGE—Oo-Ka-Yo-Sv-I S-Que-Wi ᏍᎥᎯᎡᎢ ᏌᏔᎥ

Quarter cabbage, spread it out in the loft to dry. Store in a dry place for winter. When ready to eat it should be parboiled, washed and cooked again with whatever seasoning you like and have handy.

LEATHER BREECHES—A-Ni-Ka-Yo-Sv-Hi Tsu-Ya DhᎥᎯᎡᎠ ᎫᏔ

Break beans and string on a thread, hang in the sun or warm place to dry. To prepare they should be parboiled, washed, removed from the string and cooked with salt or other seasoning until done.

PUMPKIN—I-Ya ᴛꙍ

Cut ripe pumpkin in rings, remove the peeling, hang on a stick before the fire near enough to dry slowly. Store this in the attic until ready for use. To prepare it should be washed and cooked any way you like pumpkin. The old Indians oftimes ate it dried without being cooked.

BLOOD PUDDING

When butchering an animal have a bucket handy with salt in the bottom to catch the blood as soon as the animal is stuck. Stir the blood to keep it from clotting. When the pouch is removed, clean it well, add a little fat to the blood as it is put into the pouch, add black pepper. Sew up the opening of the pouch, put into a pot of water and boil until done. Set aside to cool before slicing to serve.

SQUIRREL—Sa-Lo-Li ᎤᎬᏢ

Throw freshly killed squirrel into the fire to burn off the fur, remove, scrape with a knife or sharp rock. Repeat this until the squirrel is rid of all fur. Wash the squirrel well with water and wood ashes until the skin is white. Remove the insides, cook in the oven or before the fire until brown, then stew or fry until done.

RAMPS—Wa-S-Di ᎦꙴᏘ

Gather young ramps soon after they come up. Parboil them, wash and fry in a little grease. Meal may be added if you wish. They may be cooked without being parboiled or even eaten raw if the eater is not social minded.

CRAYFISH—Ge-Tv-Nv ᏆᏢᏒ

Catch crayfish by baiting them with groundhog meat or buttermilk. Pinch off the tails and legs to use. Parboil, remove the hulls and fry the little meat that is left. When crisp it is ready to eat. May also be made into soup or stew after being fried.

GROUNDHOG—O-Ga-Na ᏍᏚᎾ

Catch groundhog, skin, parboil and make a stew. Stew may be thickened with meal.

FISH SOUP—A-Gudi Oo-Ga-Ma ᎠᏊᏗ ᎤᎦᎹ

Clean and bake fish very brown. Put into pot of water and cook until done. Serve this soup with mush.

MUSH—A-Ni-S-Ta ᎠᏂᏍᏔ

Add salt to a pot of water, boil, add cornmeal and cook until the meal is done. This is good served with meats, soups or stews. It is also good eaten by itself.

BIRD—Ge-S-Qua ᎨᏍᏆ

Clean the bird leaving it as whole as possible. Run a stick through it and roast before the fire. This is good served with mush.

MUSHROOMS—Di-Wa-Li ᏗᏩᎵ

Gather, wash, parboil, wash again to remove slimy part, fry in grease.

LARGE MUSHROOMS—Wi-Si ᏫᏏ

Wash the mushroom, parboil, wash again and fry in grease.

PHEASANTS—Tlv-Di-S-Ti ᏢᏗᏍᏘ

Dress pheasant, cook in oven or before the fire until very brown, then stew or fry until done. Good with mush.

SWAMP POTATOES—Tla-Wa-Tsu-Hi-A-Ne-Hi Nu-Nv ᏝᏩᏧᎯᎠᏁᎯ ᏄᏅ

Gather and wash swamp potatoes. Bake in oven or in ashes until they are done. Beat the cooked potatoes in the corn beater until like meal. Use as meal is used. During winter famines many Cherokees had no other meal except that made from the swamp potato.

BUTTERBEANS—Tsu-Ya Ne-Qua ᏧᏯ ᏁᏆ

The Cherokee butterbeans are very large and have purple splotches on them. They are never cooked by themselves because in that way they have a very bitter taste. They are always used in bean bread.

GRITTED BREAD

Pull the corn just past the roasting ear stage. Grit

the raw corn on a metal gritter. Add a little lye or soda and salt. Cook by baking, or make into bean bread. Extra liquid does not have to be added often because the natural milk is still in the corn.

DRIED APPLES—Oo-Ni-Ka-Yo Sv-I Sv-Ga-Ta ᏬᏂᎠᎿ ᎡᏔ ᎡᏍᏭ
Peel and quarter ripe apples, or slice them, dry in the sun. Cook until done or they may be eaten raw. Cornmeal may be added while cooking if they are to be thickened. They are good for fried pies.

FRIED BREAD
Make soft dough with flour, drop small bits in hot grease and fry until brown and crisp. These are best when served hot.

SECTION FIVE

YELLOWJACKET SOUP—S-Ka-V Oo-Ga-Ma ᏬᎥᎢ
Hunt for ground-dwelling yellowjackets either in the early morning or in the late afternoon. Gather the whole comb. Place the comb over the fire or on the stove with the right side up to loosen the grubs that are not covered. Remove all the uncovered grubs. Place the comb now over the fire or on the stove upside down until the paper-like covering parches. Remove the comb from the heat, pick out the yellowjackets and place in the oven to brown. Make the soup by boiling the browned yellowjackets in a pot of water with salt and grease added if you like.

PARCHED YELLOWJACKETS
Prepare the yellowjackets as for soup but eat as soon as they are brown.

LOCUST—V-Le ᎢᎷ
Gather the locust (cicada) at night immediately after they have left their shells, wash and fry them in a small amount of grease. Eat these hot or cold. Be sure that

you gather the locust before the sun hits them or they will not be good. If you gather them before they split out of their shells they only have to be peeled to be ready to wash and fry.

GROUNDHOG—O-Ga-Na ᏍᎦᎾ

Clean a nice fat groundhog and parboil until tender. Remove from the pot, sprinkle with salt and both black and red pepper and bake before the fire or in the oven until brown.

COON—Gv-Li Ᏸ Ꮅ

Clean a coon, parboil in water with plenty of red pepper added. When tender remove from the pot and add salt and black pepper and bake brown.

OPOSSUM—Oo-Ge-S-Ti ᏍᎦᏒᎤ

Clean an opossum and parboil in plain water. Remove from pot and season with salt and pepper before browning. Most people can eat only a small amount of this because it is so greasy.

EGG SOUP—We-Gi Oo-Ga-Ma ᏪᏱ ᏍᎦᎹ

Beat eggs--chicken or bird--slightly and pour into boiling water. Season this with salt and grease, meat if you have it. Serve the soup hot with mush.

CORNBREAD SOUP—Se-Lu Ga-Du Oo-Ga-Ma ᏒᎾ ᎦᏚ ᏍᎦᎹ

Slice cold cornbread as thin as possible. Toast both sides before the fire, drop the toasted pieces into boiling water and season with grease and meat if you have it.

MEAT SKIN SOUP

Boil meat skins of any kind until they are done, bake or roast until they are brown. Put in water with a little salt and boil until you get a good flavor. Thicken with a little cornmeal, cook until cornmeal is done.

QUAIL—Gu-Que ᎫᏩ

Dress pheasant, put on a stick before the fire or over

hot coals and roast real brown. Put browned pheasant into a pot of water and boil until well done, thicken the soup with a little cornmeal and add salt. Eat by itself, with bread or with mush.

HONEY LOCUST DRINK

Gather honey locust beans when they are ripe, strip them in half lengthwise, soak in hot (not boiling) water for a while, strain this through a cloth. Sweeten the strained juice and reheat or let get cold to drink.

OLD FIELD APRICOT DRINK—Oo-Wa-Ga ᏬᎦᏏ

Gather ripe field apricots (the fruit of the Passion flower) pour hot water over them, squash out the pulp, strain this mixture through a cloth. Drink hot.

PEPPERMINT TEA

Gather peppermint--the kind that grows along the branches. Crush the leaves, pour boiling water over them and serve hot. May be sweetened if desired.

ARTICHOKES—Gv-Ge ᎬᎨ

Gather artichokes, wash off dirt and eat raw with salt.

WATERCRESS

Gather, wash, eat raw with salt or with hot grease poured over it.

RAMPS—Wa-S-Di ᎦᏍᏗ

Parboil young ramps. While they are parboiling fry some meat, put the ramps into the meat grease, add salt and fry until done.

CREASES

Pick the plant when it is tender (it is tender most of the time), wash, boil and then fry in grease.

SOCHANI—So-Cha-Ni ᏉᏣᏅᏂ

Pick plants while they are still young, parboil, wash, fry in grease.

WANEGIDUN—Wa-Ne-Gi-Dun GⱭ⅄S

Pick when tender, parboil, fry and serve with eggs and bread or just bread.

SECTION SIX

CORNMEAL GRAVY

Put some water, milk (if you have it), salt, red pepper in a skillet where meat has been cooked if you have meat, but if you don't have meat just put it in a clean skillet. Add cornmeal and cook until the meal is done. Eat this by itself or with bread for breakfast or with vegetables if you have some.

BAKED SQUIRREL

Dress a freshly killed squirrel with his skin left on. To do this you singe the fur off in the fire and then scrub the skin with ashes out of the fire. Wash the squirrel good on the inside and the outside. Rub the squirrel inside and outside with lard. Bake him before the fire or in the oven until he is well brown. Cut the squirrel up and put him in a pot, add a little water and cook until the meat is done. Add a little meal to thicken the gravy and cook until the meal is done.

SECTION SEVEN

SUCCOTASH—I-Ya-Tsu-Ya-Di-Su-Yi Se-Lu TꙎꙂꙎ˞Ⱶ 4M

Shell some corn, skin it with wood ashes lye. Cook corn and beans separately, then together. If desired you may put pieces of pumpkin in, be sure to put the pumpkin in in time to get done before the pot is removed from the fire.

SECTION EIGHT

PARCHED CORN

Put hot ashes in a basket or a pot, put in some corn, stir until the corn is brown. Clean ashes off with a dry cloth or leaves, beat the corn in the corn beater. Make soup from the large particles of cracked corn by stirring it in boiling water until it is done.

This kind of parched corn and parched corn soup would often be used on the hunt, the corn being carried wrapped in a piece of skin to be eaten dry or to be made into soup. This was really all that was needed to be carried from home when the Cherokees went on a hunt of many days.

GRITTED BREAD
Pull corn that is just a little too hard for roasting ears. Grit this corn on a homemade gritter. Make the gritted meal into bean bread or just plain bread. If the plain was baked real done it would last a whole week in most any kind of weather without souring. This kind of bread could be baked in the woods by spreading leaves of the cucumber tree on a clean spot of ground or on a stone. To cook it this way put the dough on the leaves and cover it with some more leaves and then cover the whole thing with live coals and hot ashes. Let cook until done.

FISH—A-Gu-Di   ᎠᎫᏘ
Salt cleaned fish and let stand overnight. String the salted fish on a stick the next morning and hang before the fire, turning them often to get them roasted just right. If a person was lucky to have a frying pan and some grease he could cook the fish quicker but they wouldn't taste very good.

BEAR—Yo-Na   ᏲᎾ
Cut the meat in strips and dry before the fire. Hang these dried strips across the rafters of the cabin on a basswood stick to keep dry all winter. It is best to cover the dried meat with a cloth if you have one. When you get ready to eat the bear meat take it off the stick, beat it in the beater until it is like cornmeal. Put this in a pot of plain water and boil until the soup tastes good. Eat this with mush if you want it to taste best.

MUSH—A-Ni-S-Ta   ᎠᏂᏍᏔ
Let plain water boil in a pot, wet the meal up with a

little cold water. Add the wet meal slowly to the boiling water and stir until it is done.

HOMINY SOUP

Use hominy corn to make hominy soup. Put the corn in lye until the skin slips. Beat the corn in the corn beater, sift the meal to remove the larger particles. Cook the larger particles in water until they are done. Store this soup in a pottery jar, it turns sour like buttermilk by the next day. You can keep this four days before you have to throw any of it out. This drink was always offered to visitors and enjoyed by those who worked in the field.

SWEET CORN MIXTURE—Se-Di Tsu-Ya Se-Lu 4ᴊ ᴊꚙ 4M

Skin flour corn by putting it in lye. Cook the corn until it is done, add beans and continue cooking until the beans are done, add pumpkin and cook until it is done, then add walnut meal and a little corn meal, maybe a little sugar or molasses, and cook until the corn meal is done.

WALNUT MEAL—Se-Di Se-Lu I-Sa A Su-Yi 4ᴊ 4M Tʰ D Ꮾᏸ

Crack dry walnuts and take out the meats. Beat the meats in the corn beater until they are like meal.

Old Cherokee Customs About Food

Preserving Indian Foods

Althea Bass in *"Cherokee Messenger,"* University of Oklahoma Press, Norman, Okla. 1936. pp. 55-57, makes this comment about food among the Cherokees in the 1820's (the parts in quotations are from Manuscripts of John Howard Payne. Cherokee Notes, II, p. 51. Newberry Library, Ayer Collection):

Supplies were of uncertain quantity at Brainerd (Mission). Sometimes there was an abundance of food, if an Indian friend brought them some venison or if the mission bought a "beef creature" to be butchered. They relished fresh meat, after days without it, but they put aside a thrifty portion to be cured or dried for use at a time when fresh meat was not available. Gluttony was not a habit to foster, when there were always lean days ahead.

Here are the instructions which Mrs. John Ross gave for "always having corn in fresh condition, as if freshly plucked." "The corn (flint corn in preference) to be plucked when soft & ready for roasting ears. The outer husks to be taken off, and the ears to be boiled thoroughly. The inner husks, after this, are to be drawn back so as to enable it to be tied up in bunches.

"Under a scaffolding raised on poles, it is then to be suspended over a slow fire, till it becomes perfectly dry and rather smoked. It may be some days in undergoing this preparation. When thoroughly dry, it must be removed, and hung in a dry place so as not to mould.

"When wanted for use, the grains must be shelled & boiled over again. At first it will be found shrunken & as hard as stone; but cooking will bring it out fresh & soft."

Observations on the Creek and Cherokee Indians
By William Bartram in 1789

From *Transaction of the American Ethnological Society* Vol. 3 Pt. 1
EXTRACTS:

They use a strong lixivium prepared from Ashes of bean stalks and other vegetables in all their food prepared from corn, which otherwise, they say, breeds worms in their stomachs.

The vines or climbing stems of the climber (Bigonia Crucigera) are equally divided longitudinally into four parts by the same number of their membranes, somewhat resembling a piece of white tape, by which means, when the vine is cut through and divided traversely, it presents to view the likeness of a cross. This membrane is of a sweet, pleasant taste. The country people of Carolina crop these vines to pieces, together with china brier and sassafras roots, and boil them in their beer in the spring, for diet drink, in order to attenuate and purify the blood and juices. It is a principal ingredient in Howards famous infusion for curing the yaws, etc., the virtues and use of which he obtained from Indian Doctors.

Their animal food consists chiefly of venison, bears' flesh, turkeys, hares, wild fowl, and domestic poultry; and also of domestic kind, as beeves, goats and swine—never horse flesh, though they have horses in great plenty; neither do they eat the flesh of dogs, cats or any such creatures as are rejected by white people. Their vegetable food consists chiefly of corn, rice, convelvulus batatas, or those nourishing roots usually called the sweet or spanish potatoes (but in the Creek country they never eat the Irish potato).

All the species of the phaeolus and dolichos in use among the whites, are cultivated by the Creeks, Cherokees, etc. and make up a great part of their food.

All the species of Cucurbita, as squashes, pumpkins, watermelons, etc., but of the cucumeres, they cultivate none of the species as yet, neither do they cultivate our farinaceous grains, as wheat, barley, spelts, rye, buckwheat, etc. (not having got the use of the plow amongst them, though it has been introduced some years ago). The chiefs rejected it, alleging that it would starve their old people who employed themselves in planting, and selling their produce, and selling their produce to the traders, for their support and maintenance; seeing that by permitting the traders to use the plow, one or two persons could easily raise more grain than all the old people of the town could do by using the hoe. Turnips, parsnips, salads, etc. they had no knowledge of.

But besides the cultivated fruits above recited, with peaches, oranges, plums (Chickasaw Plums), figs, and some apples, they have in use a vast variety of wild or native vegetables, both fruits and roots, viz: diospyros, morus rubra, gleditsia, miltiloba, s. tricanthus; all the species of juglans and acorns, from which they extract a very sweet oil, which enters into all their cooking; and several species of palms, which furnish them a great variety of agreeable and nourishing food. Grapes, too, they have in great variety and abundance, which they feed on occasionally when ripe; they also prepare them for keeping and lay up for winter and spring time (Vitis Vinifera; I call them so because they approach, as respects the largeness of the fruit and their shape and flavor, much nearer the grapes of Europe and Asia, of which wine is made, and are especially different from our wild grapes, and as different from the fox or bull grape of Penn. and Carolina.)

A species of smilax (s. pseudochina) affords them a delicious and nourishing food, which is prepared from its vast, tuberous roots. They dig up these roots, and while yet fresh and full of juice, chop them into pieces, and them-macerate them well in wooden mortars; this substance they put in vessels nearly filled with clean water, when, being mixed well with paddles, whilst the finer parts are yet floating in the liquid, they decant it off into other vessels, leaving the farinaceous substance at the bottom, which, being taken out and dried is an impalpable powder or farina, of a reddish color. Then when mixed in boiling water, becomes a beautiful jelly, which sweetened with honey or sugar, affords a most nourishing food for children or aged people; or when mixed with fine corn flour, and fried in fresh bear's grease, makes excellent fritters.

Examples of Uses of Cherokee Foods by People Elsewhere

Quoting from a letter written by Dr. Karl Blyel of Union College, Barbourville, Ky. we have this account of the use made of Cherokee recipes and foods at the Daniel Boone Festival of 1949 and 1950:

"Each year during the third week in October we start off our Daniel Boone Festival with a Cherokee Banquet. It is held on Thursday evening. It is given to honor the Cherokee Indians who are present in full regalia. The program is put on partly by Cherokees and partly by whites. The food is entirely Cherokee and is prepared after the recipes obtained from the Cherokees. We do not, of course, prepare the foods as the old timers did, but must use simplified techniques. Bean Bread and Indian Corn are two of our favorites. These are again (for 1951) on the menu. Quite a few people around here now use the Indian corn recipe as well as some of the other recipes. I've had numerous requests for some of the recipes used at the banquets. Our menu is always in Cherokee, using English letters. Last year (1950) we turned away 40 people at the door of the banquet hall, these had hoped that there would be some cancelled reservations."

It might be of interest to many to know that another important part of the Daniel Boone Festival is the signing of the Cane Treaty, a treaty by which the Cherokees are given free access to a quantity of cane in the area surrounding Barbourville.

NATIVE HERBS

And Some of the Uses Made of Them By the Cherokee People

Spignet	Backache	Make tea or powder of the roots
Rabbit Tobacco	Colds	Make tea of leaves and stalks
Red Alder	High blood	Make tea of bark
Wild Cherry	Measles and colds	Make tea of bark
Beech Bark	Vomiting	Make tea
Peach Leaves	Boils and risings	Make poultice from leaves and meal
Boneset	Pneumonia	Make tea of leaves and stalks
Small Ragweed	Poison oak or ivy	Heat leaves and rub on
Goldenrod	Consumption	Make tea of leaves and stalk
Ratbane	Typhoid fever	Make tea of leaves and stalk
Elder	Heartburn	Make tea of bark
Ginseng	Colic	Make tea of the roots
12 O'clock Weed	Kills flies	Crush leaves in sweet milk
Queen of the Meadow	Nausea at certain times	Make tea of leaves and roots
Christmas Fern	Fever	Make tea of leaves or stems
Ground Ivy	Hives	Make tea of leaves or stems
Yellow Root	Sore mouth, sore throat, or stomach trouble.	Make tea of the roots
Heat Leaves	Cold	Beat the whole plant and make tea
Bull Nettle	Stop teething babies from slobbering	Make beads of roots

CHEROKEE INDIAN FEAST
CHEROKEE, N. C.

Sunday, December 4th, 1949, 1 P. M.

PARCHED CORN
(Se-lu-di-gv-wi-sv-hi)

Wild Fruits

BLACKBERRIES
(Ka-nu-ga-li)
HUCKLEBERRIES
(Ka-wa-yaw)
STRAWBERRIES
(A-nu)
RASPBERRIES
(Sv-di-wa-li)
ELDERBERRIES
(Go-ga-sa-ga)
WILD PLUM
(Qua-nu-na-sti-ga)
WILD CHERRIES
(Ta-ya)
CRAB APPLES
(Sv-ga-ta Tsu-na-sdi-ga)
GROUND CHERRIES
(U-nu-gu-hi-sdi)
PERSIMMON
(Sa-li)
FIELD APRICOTS
(U-wa-go)
FALL GRAPES
(Te-lv-la-di)
FOX GRAPES
(Qua-lu-si)
OPOSSUM GRAPES
(U-ni-na-su-ga)
DEWBERRIES
(U-da-si-nu-da)
GOOSEBERRIES
(A-ya-lo-ti-sgi)

Nuts

HICKORY NUTS
(So-hi)
HAZELNUTS
(Yu-gi-dv)
WALNUTS
(Se-di)
BUTTERNUTS
(Go-hi)

Drinks

SUMACADE
(Qua-lo-ga)
SASSAFRAS TEA
(Ga-na-sda-tsi)
SPICEWOOD TEA
(No-da-tsi)

Breads

CHESTNUT BREAD
(Di-squa-ni)
BEAN BREAD
(Du-ya Di-su-yi-ga-du)
HOMINY BREAD
(Di-ga-nu-le-dv-ga-du)
WILD POTATO BREAD
(I-go-di A-ne-nu-na)
FLOUR CORN BREAD
(Se-lu-yahi-ga-du)
SWEET POTATO BREAD
(Nu-nv-a-su-yl-ga-du)
MOLASSES BREAD
(Wa-du-li-si-ga-du)

Meats

ROAST BEAR
(Yo-na-a-wi-ya Sv-na-ta-nu-hi)
ROAST DEER
(A-wi-A-wi-ya Sv-na-ta-nu-hi)
SPECKLED TROUT
(A-na-dv-tsi)
ROAST BISON
(Ya-na-sa Sv-na-ta-nu-hi)
MUSHROOMS
(U-ni-lo-que)
RACCOON
(Gv-li)
TURKEY
(Gv-na-ga-la-gi-na)

Vegetables

POTATOES
(Nu-na)
CORN
(Se-lu)
HOMINY
(A-ma-ge-i)
BEANS
(Du-ya)
WILD GREENS
(So-tsv-na)
PUMPKIN
(I-ya)
SUCCOTASH
(Se-lu-du-ya-di-su-yi)
ARTICHOKE
(Gv-tsi)
RAMPS
(Wa-sdi)

Sponsored by
THE MUSEUM OF THE CHEROKEE INDIAN

For Palefaces

By WALTER CARROLL, Sunday writer

Photos by Warner Ogden except of bogeyman dance, which is by K. J. Shepard.

Durham Morning Herald, December 11, 1949

THE handsome Cherokee Indians of Western North Carolina will probably be eating leftovers for the next few weeks, if the appetites of the many white people who attended their Second Annual Feast at the reservation in Cherokee last Sunday were any indication. A few whites at our table, their faces registering various expressions, ate some of the food; most of them just played around with it. The Indians, running true to form, cleaned up their plates.

The occasion, in addition to the great feast, sponsored by the Museum of the Cherokee Indian, was the 18th meeting of the North Carolina Anthropological and Archaeological Society which convened there last Saturday. Another event was the presentation of a Sequoya tree to Chief Bradley, who accepted it on behalf of the Indians on the reservation.

In making the presentation talk Mr. Beck said, "Chief Bradley, in behalf of the Museum of the Cherokee Indian and in collaboration with the U. S. Forest Service and the University of California, I present to your loving care a small plant of the Giant Sequoia, symbol of the oldest living thing upon this earth.

"It was indeed fitting that these, the noblest of trees, with their massive red trunks, should honor one of our original Americans, and a Cherokee Indian.

"Today, in presenting to you this tree, we pay tribute to George Gist, or Sequoyah, who in 1821 had developed an alphabet of 86 symbols representing each sound in the language of the tribe, which was so simple that anyone in the tribe could quickly learn to read and write. It was considered one of the cultural masterpieces of modern times and the means of diffusing to his Cherokee people the wonders of books and literature which increased their love and appreciation of the beauty of the world in which they lived.

"Chief Bradley, plant this tree, and may it ever grow beneath the noon-day sun of a North Carolina bright blue sky as a fitting symbol of the noble character of the Cherokee Cadmus whose name it honors.

"May the songs played by the winds over its foliage and the poetry read from the lips of the passing waters of the Ocona Luftee river join this tree in keeping forever fresh and green the memory of Sequoyah."

FOR THE FIRST TIME IN MANY MOONS, roast Buffalo was eaten by the Cherokee Indians and others at the second annual Cherokee Indian Feast at the Cherokee Indian Reservation in the Great Smokies. Chief Carl Standingdeer sits at end of table, while a line of guests behind them walks past a long table loaded with 46 different foods, to select what they want, cafeteria-style. Buffalo was flown in from Wyoming.

Samuel Francis Allison of Brevard, wearing "Genius at Work" apron, who prepared the roast bear, roast buffalo and other meats is shown with Indian cooks who prepared 46 foods at the second annual Cherokee Indian Feast.

Mrs. Lula Sequoya, with 5 month old papoose on back, steps up to Cherokee Indian Feast table for a serving of roast buffalo, bear and anything else she wanted from the 46 foods. Samuel Allison from Brevard who prepared the Roast Meats, is holding the ladle.

The invocation was offered by the Reverend Ben Bushyhead, a Cherokee minister, in the Cherokee tongue.

Indian cooks from every section of the 63,000-acre reservation prepared the feast, using recipes that had been handed down for hundreds of years. Spread out on a long table in the Student's Dining Hall were roast bear, venison, bison, speckled trout, mushrooms, raccoon and wild turkey. There were chestnut bread, bean bread, hominy bread, wild potato bread, flour corn bread, sweet potato bread and molasses bread.

Vegetables included potatoes, corn, hominy, beans, wild greens, pumpkin, succotash, artichoke and ramps. The drinks included sumac-ade, a delicious pink colored drink, sassafras tea, spicewood tea and hickorynut milk.

Wild fruits included blackberries, huckleberries, strawberries, raspberries, elderberries, wild plum, wild cherries, crab apples, ground cherries, persimmon, field apricots, fall grapes, fox grapes, opossum grapes, dewberries and gooseberries.

Still hungry? Hickory nuts, hazel nuts, walnuts, chestnuts and butternuts were also on the bill of fare.

This reporter found most of the meal very enjoyable. The bear meat served in roast style was very good, so was the bison and venison but the hominy and hickory nut mixture the Cherokees can keep. The spicewood tea, although it smelled like an expensive brand of perfume, was also good. The strange foods were too much for *Herald* city editor Russell Brantley. He sniffed, tasted, then ate no more. This writer consumed his bear, bison and deer meat. Warner Ogden, *Knoxville News Sentinel* state editor and *Life* magazine correspondent, ate everything on his plate. He explained he had eaten the food before. The Indian sitting next to Ogden cleaned up his plate. K. T. Sheperd, president of the Virginia Archaeological Society ate almost all of his food. A young ethnologist sitting across the table pushed his food away, saying, "I think I'll stick to the study of their origin, distribution, relations and peculiarities." Mr. and Mrs. Herbert Wentworth of Durham also attended the feast. The drinks were served by Cherokee Indian School girls. Guests from as far away as the Great Lakes to Manteo and from New England to the Gulf of Mexico attended the feast.

Indian does bogeyman dance wearing a rare mask. Those sitting take their turn. Man on extreme right is 77-year-old Nickajack George wearing a wildcat face. These rare masks were worn for first time in many years.

Samuel E. Beck presided and introduced H. E. Wheeler, director of the Museum, who was master of ceremonies. Joe Jennings, superintendent of the Cherokee Reservation, made a short address of welcome which was followed by the address of the honor guest, Dr. Arthur Kelly, head of the department of anthropology, University of Georgia.

The Curator

Harry Edgar Wheeler, born in Birmingham, Alabama, was educated at Lehigh and Vanderbilt Universities. For many years he was a staff member of the Field Museum (now the Chicago Museum of Natural History). He has been curator of the Alabama Museum of Natural History at the University of Alabama and has done special work for the University of Arkansas, Witte Museum, and the Maltbie-Beal Shell Museum. He is author of the "Birds of Arkansas" and also a biography of Timothy Abbot Conrad, the paleontologist, and many contributions to scientific journals in the fields of ornithology, paleontology, mineralogy and philately.

Problem of Cherokee Origin

Dr. Kelly explained that his initial concern with Cherokee origins occured when he came to the Cherokee reservation in 1929 as a fellow of the National Research Council. He had traveled from Harvard to make a racial study of the present tribes, principally their head forms, which are dolichocephalic, in contrast he said, with most southeastern tribes, who were prevailingly round-headed.

"Speculations about the origins of the Cherokee" Dr. Kelly said, "have agitated the minds of anthropologists for fifty years or more, beginning with James Mooney, who made investigations on Cherokee myths and traditions at the turn of the century."

"Anthropologists", Dr. Kelly told the people gathered at the feast, "have always been intrigued by the ethnic picture of the Cherokee, holding the great central massif of the Southern Appalachian Mountains, a mountain people whose culture always reflected adaptation to the uplands, surrounded by tribes of different linguistic and cultural backgrounds. To the south and west, since earliest recorded history (the reports of the expedition of Hernando De Soto and other 16th century Spanish explorers) were the various tribes belonging to the great Muskogean-speaking family. On the north were the Algonquins and Iroquoian relatives, and toward the Carolina coast was the conclave of Siouian-speaking tribes, whose presence as detached Siouian tribes in the southeast is almost as big a mystery as the Cherokees."

68

Dr. Kelly explained that archaeologically the picture of the Cherokee origins remain a mystery despite the great amount of theorizations. This is true, he said, in spite of the extensive archaeological work done in the southeast in the last 20 years. Work of the Tennessee Department of Anthropology, Dr. Kelly stated, has indicated that the over-hill Cherokees were culturally divergent from the parent body of the older Cherokee settlements in the highland sections of North Carolina and South Carolina.

Dr. Kelly was high in his praise of the Cherokee people. He described them as a brave, wise and intelligent group, but added that they had always been "Something like the Irish" in that they could not pass up a good fight when they saw one.

The Museum of the Cherokee Indian

The Museum of the Cherokee Indian, founded by Samuel E. Beck, is one of the most interesting of its kind in the country.

Mr. Beck makes his home in Asheville, N. C., where he is Credit and Office Manager for Armour and Company. He is a descendent of John Beck, the pioneer who took up land on the Ocona Luftee River within the present Smoky Park boundary shortly after the year 1800. He grew up in the heart of the Cherokee country where perhaps the spore seed came into being for his later very worthy idea of a museum.

Burnham S. Colburn for more than twenty years collected Cherokee Indian relics, acquiring the finest collections and specimens that were known to exist. In addition, he opened up many mounds in various sections of the Cherokee country and in all his collecting he followed the advice and direction of the Smithsonian Institution. Mr. Beck was a guest in the Colburn home and saw the collection and later met Dr. Neil M. Judd, curator of the archaeological division of the Smithsonian and learned from him that they considered Mr. Colburn's collection of Cherokee artifacts the largest in existence.

Mr. Beck had an impulse to acquire the collection and send it back to the Cherokee country, there to be preserved forever as a monument to their ancient culture.

The collection was acquired and the Museum opened in May, 1948. Since that time it has been a policy of the Museum to acquire, find, purchase and preserve any examples of Cherokee relics or workmanship from the most ancient down to modern times. Recent acquisitions have been the Kirksey collection of Union Mills, North Carolina; the Weatherby collection of Grant, Virginia; the late Dr. Frank Speck collection and many individual items from the Cherokees on the Reservation. There are now more than 50,000 different Cherokee artifacts belonging to the Museum.

The library of the Museum is devoted exclusively to books, manuscripts and papers relating to the Cherokee Indian. It is constantly growing, and in it may be found the works of the earlier travelers among the Cherokee like Bartram, Lawson and Adair, Congressional and Senatorial documents, Cherokee literature in Sequoya characters such as the Cherokee *Bible*, the *New Testament*, The Cherokee Constitution, *The Cherokee Messenger* all issues complete, *The Cherokee Advocate, Cherokee Phoenix, Memoirs of Catharine Brown* and the *Memoirs of Narcissa Owen*. The student will find for research purposes the above and many other rare books, papers and documents concerning the Cherokee.

MRS. SAMUEL E. BECK makes traditional Cherokee drink (Qua-lo-ga) with berries of red sumach. Berries are shelled off and rubbed gently between the palms of the hands being careful not to crush the berries but only the spines, drop into water, strain, sweeten to taste, cool and serve.

INDEX

70

COACHWHIP PUBLICATIONS

COACHWHIPBOOKS.COM

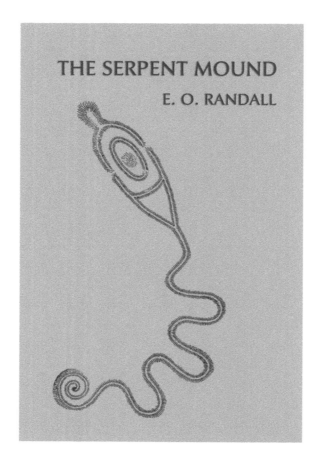

The Serpent Mound
ISBN 1-61646-167-5

COACHWHIP PUBLICATIONS

ALSO AVAILABLE

Drums, Tomtoms, and Rattles
ISBN 1-61646-162-4

Coachwhip Publications

CoachwhipBooks.com

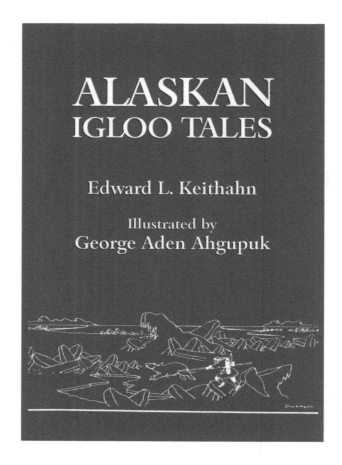

ALASKAN
IGLOO TALES

Edward L. Keithahn

Illustrated by
George Aden Ahgupuk

Alaskan Igloo Tales
ISBN 1-61646-199-3

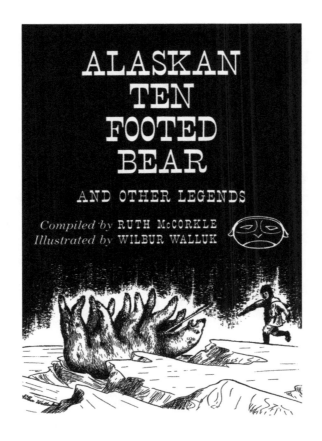

Alaskan Ten-Footed Bear and Other Legends
ISBN 1-61646-201-9

COACHWHIP PUBLICATIONS

COACHWHIPBOOKS.COM

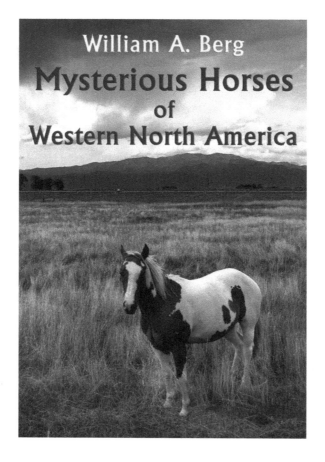

Mysterious Horses of Western North America
ISBN 1-61646-027-X

COACHWHIP PUBLICATIONS

ALSO AVAILABLE

The Last Mammoth
ISBN 1-61646-245-0

COACHWHIP PUBLICATIONS

COACHWHIPBOOKS.COM

KATHARINE LUOMALA
THE MENEHUNE
OF POLYNESIA
AND OTHER MYTHICAL LITTLE PEOPLE OF OCEANIA

The Menehune of Polynesia
ISBN 1-61646-214-0

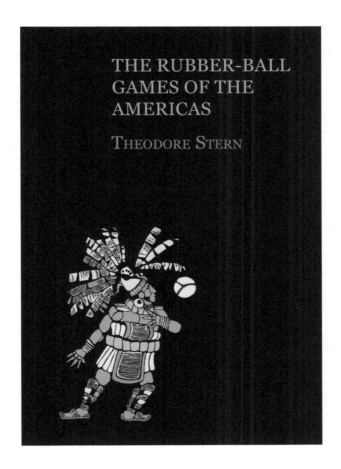

The Rubber Ball Games of the Americas
ISBN 1-61646-210-8

Printed in the USA
CPSIA information can be obtained
at www.ICGtesting.com
LVHW071512271023
762325LV00012B/257